Contents

1. Happy ever after?   4

2. Getting along   6

3. When things go wrong   10

4. How it feels   24

5. Splitting up   32

6. Moving on   42

Glossary   46
Further information   47
Index   48

1. Happy ever after?

A perfect start?

It's Kim and Adam's wedding day. All their family and friends have come to celebrate and wish them well for the future. They both have many hopes and dreams for their lives together. Whatever happens, they are sure they will face the future together and grow old side by side. But will they really live happily ever after?

When people get married, they hope their marriage is going to last forever. However, they must also face the fact that marriages today often end in divorce. In many parts of the world, one in three couples do not manage to stay together.

▶ *Every married couple hopes that they'll always be happy together.*

6·99

Why do families break up?

Jane Bingham

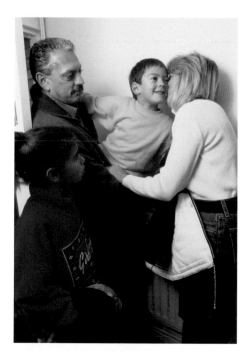

HODDER
Wayland

TOWER HAMLETS COLLEGE
Learning Centre
Poplar High Street
LONDON
E14 0AF

an imprint of Hodder Children's Books

Other titles in this series:
Why are people racist?
Why are people refugees?
Why are people terrorists?
Why are people vegetarian?
Why do people abuse human rights?
Why do people bully?
Why do people commit crime?
Why do people drink alcohol?
Why do people fight wars?
Why do people gamble?
Why do people harm animals?
Why do people join gangs?
Why do people live on the streets?
Why do people smoke?
Why do people take drugs?

For more information on this series and other Hodder
Wayland titles, go to www.hodderwayland.co.uk

Editor: Philip de Ste. Croix
Cover design: Hodder Children's Books
Inside design: Clare Nicholas
Consultant: Paula Hall, Youth Counsellor and
   Couples Counsellor, Relate
Picture research: Shelley Noronha – Glass Onion
   Pictures
Indexer: Amanda O'Neill

Published in Great Britain in 2004 by Hodder
Wayland, an imprint of Hodder Children's Books.
This paperback edition published in 2006

British Library Cataloguing in Publication Data
Bingham, Jane
   Why do families break up?
   1. Divorce - Juvenile literature 2. Family -
   Juvenile literature
   I. Title II. De Ste. Croix, Philip

ISBN-10: 0 7502 4829 7
ISBN-13: 987 0 7502 4829 7

Printed in China

Hodder Children's Books
A division of Hodder Headline Limited
338 Euston Road, London NW1 3BH

Picture acknowledgements
The publisher would like to thank the following
for their kind permission to use their pictures:
John Birdsall Social Issues Photo Library 11; Corbis
(cover), Angela Hampton Family Life Picture Library
(imprint page), 5, 6, 7, 8, 15, 22, 24, 31, 32, 34, 35, 38,
39, 44; Hodder Wayland Picture Library (contents)
(top) (Jeff Isaac Greenberg), (contents) (bottom), 9,
13, 14, 17, 23, 25, 27, 30, 42 (Jeff Isaac Greenberg), 45
(Jeff Isaac Greenberg); Photofusion 20 (Emma Smith);
Skjold Photos 40; Topham/ImageWorks 4, 10 (Bob
Collins), 12 (Esbin/Anderson), 16 (Bob Daemmrich),
18, 19 (Nancy Richmond), 21 (Eastcott/Momatiuk), 26
(Michael Siluk), 28 (Michael Siluk), 29 (Nancy
Richmond), 33 (Bob Daemmrich), 36, 37 (Monika
Graff), 43 (Dion Ogust); Topham/Photri 41.

Cover picture: Father and son in a home office.

Divorce figures are rising all the time and marriages are lasting for shorter and shorter periods. Some couples may survive a break-up without too much suffering, but for most families the experience of splitting up is very painful. During the time that a relationship is falling apart, all the members of the family suffer. After the split, some parents will not see as much of their children as they would like, and the children will no longer live in a nuclear family.

So why do so many families break up? This book looks at some of the reasons why relationships fall apart, and examines how the experience feels from the children's point of view.

▲ *Not all marriages last a lifetime. Breaking up can be a very lonely time for everyone involved.*

FACT:
In the year 2000, experts estimated that approximately 50 per cent of all marriages in the United States were likely to end in divorce, so that for every two marriages there was one divorce. In the UK and Australia, the figure is around 40 per cent, with two in five marriages not lasting beyond 15 years. In the UK, it is estimated that around 40 per cent of the present generation of children will experience their parents divorcing or separating before they are 18.

2. Getting along

Making it work

At some point in their lives, many adults make the decision that they want to share their life with someone else. They may get married or decide to live together without being married. Either way, settling down together is a very big step.

Sharing your life with someone else isn't easy, but it can be very rewarding. Many couples manage to have fun together for years, enjoying the good times, and helping each other through difficulties as well. No matter what happens, they manage to stay really good friends. So how do they do it?

▼ *Many couples never stop enjoying the fun and closeness of being together.*

One thing that can make a big difference in a relationship is communication. If one partner is sad or angry, or just needs some time on their own, it often helps if they talk to their partner about their feelings, instead of bottling everything up inside themselves.

Living with someone every day is quite a challenge. No one can look fantastic and be in a good mood all the time, and it's important for people to be realistic about their daily life together. However well two people get along together, there will always be some things about one another that they find annoying. But talking together calmly about the things they find difficult can be helpful.

Being happy together doesn't mean that people have to spend all their time in each other's company. Everyone needs to have their own friends and 'space', and the freedom to pursue their own interests. Many couples choose to spend some time apart doing something they enjoy, but this doesn't stop them having lots of fun when they're together.

"

'I think of Meg as my best friend, we get on really well together, and have lots of fun with our friends and the kids. But we don't spend all our free time together. I still go cycling a lot and Meg plays in her band.'
Steve, married to Meg for 18 years, with three children

"

▶ *Couples don't have to spend all their time together. Sometimes it's good to do something just for you!*

Good times, bad times

In any relationship, it's important to concentrate on the good things about being together. One way that couples and families can really enjoy each other's company is by making the opportunity to have some fun together every day.

Having fun can be as simple as sharing a funny story about what has happened during the day, or all getting together to watch a favourite TV programme. Celebrating special occasions and going on outings and holidays all help couples and families to enjoy each other's company and make them feel that they belong together.

However, life can't always be fun and even the happiest families go through difficult times.

▲ *Family holidays are a great time for having fun together.*

Sometimes, one partner may be under a lot of strain. They may be unhappy at work, or worried about money, or someone close to them may have died. When someone is unhappy and stressed, they can lose their temper easily and snap at the people around them.

At times like this, the other members of the family need to be very understanding. Even if they want to shout back, they need to think about why the person is behaving as they are, and try to be sympathetic. Once a couple has got through a difficult period, they can look back and feel proud that they have faced the problem together. They will probably realize that this has made their relationship stronger.

Sadly, some bad times go on for a very long while and it just doesn't seem possible to make things better.

▲ *When someone in the family is worried or under a lot of strain, everyone needs to be extra-understanding.*

case study · case study · case study · case study · case study

When Sam was 10, his family moved to a new town. His Dad was very busy in his new job, and came home really tired each night. His Mum couldn't find any interesting work and missed her old friends. When Sam went to bed, he heard his parents shouting at each other. They were both unhappy and took it out on each other. For a while, Sam was scared that that his parents would break up. But eventually, they decided to support each other, instead of feeling angry and alone. Gradually, things got better. His Dad became less stressed, his Mum found a new job, and the family started having fun together again.

3. When things go wrong

Different dreams

When two people get married or decide to live together, the last thing they think about is splitting up. But gradually they may discover that their life together is just not working out the way they had hoped.

It's good sometimes to be independent, but some couples discover that they want very different things out of life.

After a couple has been together for a while, one or both of them may begin to think that they have made a mistake. They may discover that their partner is very different from the person they thought they were marrying. This sometimes happens when people get married in a hurry. Often, couples in this situation try very hard to get along, but then one partner may decide that it would be better for both of them if they separated. The other partner may also agree.

case study · case study · case study · case study · case study

Leon and Martha started going out together when they were 16 and got married when they were 19. But by the time they were 22 they realized that they wanted very different things. Martha wanted to travel around the world, but Leon wanted to settle down and have a family. They had completely different friends and spent less and less time together. Eventually, they both agreed that they should split up.

▶ *Couples who get engaged when they are young sometimes find that they grow apart as they get older.*

Sometimes, couples get together when they are still very young. Then, as they grow older, they develop different interests. Eventually, they realize that they no longer have very much in common.

If a couple is very unhappy together they may decide that the best thing to do is to split up. Today, it's much easier to get a divorce than it was a few generations ago, and couples are not blamed so much for breaking up.

Quarrels and arguments

Some couples agree to part without too many disagreements, but for most people there is a long and painful period of rows and arguments before they split up. Of course, everyone has disagreements, and rows can be very useful for clearing the air. But when people get really angry with each other all the time it is usually a sign that they are unhappy about their lives together.

weblinks

For more information about how children feel when their parents argue, go to www.waylinks.co.uk/series/why/familybreakup

▼ *When an argument starts, people can say all sorts of hurtful things to each other.*

When couples are unhappy together they can argue about almost anything – how they spend their time, which friends they see, even which programmes they watch on TV. One subject that often causes arguments is money. A lot of couples disagree about how much money they should spend and what they should be spending it on. In many families, one or both partners feel under a lot of pressure to earn more money. They put in long hours at work and, when they get home, they are often tired and irritable.

Sometimes, one partner cannot stop criticizing the other. This can easily turn into a slanging match, as each of them starts to blame the other for the things that are going wrong in their lives.

▼ *Being stuck in the middle of a row can feel really upsetting.*

In some families, parents disagree about the way they bring up their children. One parent might expect the children to be very well behaved, while the other is more relaxed. In these cases, it can be very hard for the children who are caught in the middle.

"

'In the months before Mum and Dad split up they were arguing every night. I used to hear them after I had gone to bed when they thought I was asleep. It made me feel terrible. I wished that they'd told me more about what was going on.'

Gaby, aged 12

"

Nobody's talking

Not everyone has rows. Some people have different ways of coping with unhappiness. They withdraw into themselves and don't talk about what they are feeling and thinking. This can leave their partner feeling very cut off and can be very difficult for all the family. An unhappy 'atmosphere' can build up, as if all the unsaid things are just waiting to burst out.

◀ It can be very hard to be part of a family where nobody's talking.

Non-communication doesn't have to be silent. Sometimes people simply refuse to listen to what their partner is telling them. Whenever a topic comes up that they don't like, they rapidly change the subject.

If a couple feels that they have stopped communicating with each other, they may turn to someone else instead. This may be a friend or a relative, who understands something of their situation. Sometimes this can be helpful, as the friend helps them to work out what is making them unhappy, and perhaps persuades them to talk to their partner about it.

> 'I could tell Mum and Dad weren't getting on because they just didn't talk to each other. The only person they talked to was me. I started to spend as much time out of the house as possible, just to get away from the silence.'
>
> *Luke, aged 13*

However, after a long time of trying to communicate, one or both partners may decide that they simply cannot talk to each other and it would be better if they split up. Sometimes, one partner may fall in love with someone else, and feel that this new person understands them much better than their partner does. Eventually, they may decide that they must leave their partner to go to live with the new person in their life.

▶ *When a marriage or a relationship goes wrong, some couples just stop trying to communicate with each other.*

Facing difficulties

Sooner or later, many families have to face challenges and problems. One partner may lose their job or become ill. The family may have to move to another part of the country, or even abroad, or a family member, such as a grandparent, may die. These situations put pressure on a relationship, but usually the difficulties can be overcome. However, if a couple is not getting on, the problem can make things worse and drive them further apart.

Money worries put a great strain on families. If one partner is fired from their job, or if they have a business that goes bankrupt, it can be hard for their partner not to blame them for the difficulties that the family is suffering. Even in cases where no one is to blame – if one partner is made redundant or if they simply cannot find a job – there are still problems to deal with as the family struggles to manage with very little money.

▼ *These workers have just learned that their factory is closing down. Losing their jobs will put a big strain on their families.*

Illness can also make life difficult. If one partner becomes seriously ill, the other has to take on more responsibility. The person who is still fit and well may feel that their partner has been changed by their illness and doesn't seem the same as the person they had married.

weblinks

For more information about an organization that helps couples who are having marriage difficulties, go to www.waylinks.co.uk/series/why/familybreakup

The death of a family member can have a shattering effect on all the family, as each of them tries to come to terms with the loss in their own way. Sometimes, instead of sharing their sadness, people can withdraw into themselves and become cut off from the rest of the family.

▲ *Sometimes, when a family member such as a grandparent dies, it can make everyone in the family feel very alone.*

"

'Granny lived just round the corner from us and we used to see her every day. When she died we were all really upset, but Mum went to pieces. She couldn't stop crying and stayed in all the time. After a few weeks, Dad thought Mum ought to be getting over it, but she said she couldn't and they started to argue. It was awful, missing Granny and seeing my parents quarrelling all the time.'
Ellie, aged 10

"

17

New challenges

Moving house can be an exciting new challenge, but it can also put families under a lot of pressure. There is a great deal of work involved in packing up all your possessions and settling in somewhere new, even if it is only round the corner. But when families have to move a long way away, it can be hard for everyone.

When a family moves house, everyone has new things to get used to. If one or both parents are starting a new job, they may be worried about how they will cope, and all the family will miss their old friends and neighbours. At times like this, it is easy to blame a partner when things go wrong. Just when families need to support each other most, they may feel instead that they are falling apart.

▲ *Moving house can be very exciting, but it can also cause a lot of stress and lead to family arguments.*

Usually, the birth of a new baby is a very happy event which brings the family closer together, but in some families, having a new baby can cause a lot of stress. Often, both parents are very tired. The couple may be worried about how they will cope, and concerned that there isn't enough money to go round. The other children in the family may also have problems getting used to the baby. While everyone is telling them how happy they must be, the family may actually be feeling unhappy and worried.

▲ As well as coping with a new baby, parents often need to reassure their other children, who can be feeling very left out.

'After Cary was born, Alan wanted us to move house again. We'd moved around the country for the last ten years as Alan took new jobs working in hotels. The kids were tired of changing schools and I was just worn out. I told him that I'd had enough and I was going to stay put.'

Julie, married to Alan for 12 years, with four children

Major problems

Some families have major difficulties to cope with. One or both parents may be addicted to drugs or drink, or there may be problems of violence in the home. Serious problems like these are hard to solve without lots of encouragement and help, so most people benefit from the help of skilled professionals, such as social workers and counsellors.

▼ *Some people start drinking too much alcohol because they are feeling depressed. This can be very hard for their partners to deal with.*

Sometimes, one partner may become addicted to drugs or alcohol after a couple has been married for a while. Or they may already have had a problem before the couple got together. As time goes on, the problem may become increasingly serious until one partner feels that they just cannot cope with it any more.

Some people repeatedly hurt and abuse their partners, and even the children in the family. This is a terrifying experience for the whole family. It is very important in these situations that the victims of violence do not suffer in silence. Women who are abused by violent partners should contact their local women's refuge, which can offer them a safe place to stay. Children should also seek out help by talking to a teacher, a doctor or a relative. In most cases, teachers and doctors are required by law to help an abused child find support and advice. There are also helplines, such as Childline in the UK, which children can telephone if they are worried or frightened by any situation at home.

Sometimes, it is just too dangerous for families to stay together, and they realize that their only real chance of safety is to split up. But this does not stop families from feeling very sad that their life together has not worked out.

▲ *If a person is being abused, it is vital that they find someone to help them. This woman is at a refuge for victims of domestic violence.*

FACT:
Alcohol abuse has a dramatic effect on marriage. Experts in the UK have recorded that the divorce rate is twice as high in marriages where one partner drinks heavily as in those without any alcohol problems.

weblinks

For more information about an organization that helps children who are worried about violence in their family, go to www.waylinks.co.uk/series/why/familybreakup

Counselling can help

Sometimes, couples or families who are having problems decide to see a counsellor. Counsellors are specially trained to recognize difficulties in relationships and to help people work through their problems.

If a couple is not communicating well, a counsellor can encourage them to talk and listen to each other. Counsellors can help couples to explore their problems together and work out what they really want.

Many couples find that counselling helps them to stay together. Once they start to work through their problems, they may begin to enjoy their life together again. However, others decide that they need to split up. When a couple is separating, a counsellor can help them to talk to each other calmly and work out the best way for them to part. This help is especially valuable when children are involved.

▲ Counsellors are specially trained to help couples to talk about their problems and encourage them to communicate better.

In some cases, the whole family may see the counsellor, and children may be encouraged to talk about their feelings. This can be very helpful, especially in families where no one is talking very much.

Quite often, a young person may choose to see a counsellor on their own to talk about their feelings and the problems they are experiencing because their parents are splitting up. It can be a great comfort to talk to someone who has lots of experience and who understands what you are going through.

weblinks

For more information about an organization that provides support for families in the process of separating, go to www.waylinks.co.uk/series/why/familybreakup

▼ *Talking to someone about what's worrying you can be a great relief.*

Sad and angry

◄ *Many young people feel sad and tearful in the early stages of a family break-up.*

When the children of separating parents first realize that their Mum and Dad are splitting up, it is usual for them to feel a mixture of emotions. Over the first few weeks and months, their feelings will probably keep on changing. One minute they might feel very sad that the way of life they have known for so long is coming to an end. They may want to cry or just be quiet on their own. The next minute they might feel angry with their parents for letting them down. They may feel like shouting, or asking what they have done to deserve all this? Some of the time they might feel lost and frightened, and worried about what will happen to them in the future.

weblinks

For more information about coping with divorce and separation, go to www.waylinks.co.uk/series/why/familybreakup

At this early stage, it's common to feel helpless, as if everything is out of control. But it may help to remember that lots of other young people have been through a similar experience. Many of them have found it helpful to talk to someone – perhaps a friend or a relative – who knows them really well. Some people feel better if they write down their feelings or do some drawings. Taking some exercise – going out running or kicking a ball around – can also help you to feel better and less wound up.

▼ *Sometimes, talking to a friend can really help – and just getting out and doing something active can make you feel much better.*

'When Mum told me that Dad was leaving, I felt really angry with her. I thought it was all her fault for driving him away. But after I'd calmed down a bit I realized that they'd both been unhappy for a long while. I felt very sad that we couldn't all live together any more.'
Dan, 12

I just feel numb

The news that their parents are splitting up can leave the children in the family feeling very numb. For a while they may be just too shocked to experience any emotions at all. Many young people describe the sense of being cut off from everyone around them, even their best friends. For a while, they may not be able to concentrate on their schoolwork, or enjoy the activities that they used to find fun. All of these reactions are completely normal, and, fortunately, they do not last forever. Eventually, people settle down and begin to enjoy their daily lives again.

Jodie's parents separated when she was nine. Until then, she had always enjoyed school, but suddenly she seemed to stop trying. She was rude to her teachers and avoided her friends. One of her teachers was worried about her. She talked to Jodie about the difficult time she was going through, and told Jodie that the same thing had happened to her when she was growing up. After about a term, Jodie started to find it easier to concentrate on her schoolwork, and began to have fun with her friends again.

◀ *When everything is changing at home, it's hard to concentrate on your schoolwork.*

▼ When you are going through a bad time, it can help to write down your thoughts.

Many young people find it difficult to believe that their parents are really going to part. They tell themselves that very soon their family will be back together again. But if a couple is determined to split up, it is much better for the children to face up to the situation. Then they can start to travel through their feelings until they gradually begin to feel better again.

Not everyone feels sad when their parents split up. In families where there have been a lot of rows, the children may be relieved that they no longer have to listen to arguments every day. This is a perfectly understandable reaction and children should not feel guilty if this is how they feel.

Is it my fault?

weblinks

For more information about what happens when a family splits up, go to www.waylinks.co.uk/series/why/familybreakup

It's very common for young people who are involved in a family break-up to believe that the split is somehow their fault. They wonder if their Mum and Dad might have stayed together if only they had been better behaved, or asked for less money, or simply made their parents happier. But children are not the cause of family break-ups. When a couple separates, it's the result of problems between two adults.

All families have arguments between parents and children, especially in the children's teenage years. Even in the happiest families, parents get cross about untidy bedrooms, or staying out late! But when parents are under stress, because they are not getting on well together, the rows often increase and become more serious.

▲ *When a parent leaves home, the children may blame themselves.*

Sometimes, a young person might hear their parents arguing, and notice that their name is being mentioned a lot. They may decide that their Mum and Dad are angry or upset with them. But in fact their parents are probably just trying to work out what will be best for their children.

Parents' love for their children is very different from their feelings about each other. Two adults can be disappointed in each other, and fall 'out of love', but their love for their children is unconditional. This means that they will always love their child – even if they don't always act as if they do.

▼ *It's perfectly normal for parents to have rows with their teenage children!*

> 66
> 'In the year before Mum and Dad split up Mum and I had lots of rows. She was always going on about the mess in my room and when I asked for new clothes, she went mad. When she moved out I felt really guilty – as if I had driven her away. But she told me later that she and Dad had been fighting all the time and that was why she was so stressed out with me.'
>
> *Joel, 15*
> 99

Talking it over

When families break up, many young people find it very helpful to share their thoughts and feelings with somebody else. They may decide to talk to a relative, such as a grandparent, or they may choose someone outside their family – perhaps a teacher or a counsellor. Whoever they choose, it can be very comforting to talk to someone whom they like and trust.

It's also good for young people to talk to their parents about what is going on. Sometimes this can be difficult, especially if everyone is feeling upset, but most parents will want to know what is worrying their children. It's alright to ask questions, rather than worry in silence about things like who's going to get the family pet, but you should be prepared for your Mum and Dad not to have all the answers.

weblinks

For more information and advice for children going through a family separation, go to www.waylinks.co.uk/series/why/familybreakup

▼ *Even if they seem distracted in the middle of a family break-up, your parents will want to know what's worrying you.*

Some young people share their feelings with their brothers and sisters, and some talk to their friends. It's surprising how many people have been through a family break-up, and it can be very reassuring to discover that you are not alone. Once you start talking to your friends, you may find out that some of them have experienced the same sort of feelings and worries as you.

▲ *Sharing your feelings with a friend when you are going through a bad time at home can make you feel much better.*

FACT:
In the United States a divorce is completed on average every thirteen seconds of the day. Fewer than half of America's children can expect to spend their entire childhood living with both of their biological parents in the same home.
Divorce Resource Network statistic

5. Splitting up

Early days

The early stages of splitting up can be very painful and confusing for the whole family. When one parent leaves home, it can feel sad and strange without them around. However, if there have been a lot of arguments, it is sometimes a relief for everyone that the quarrels are over. Sometimes, the parent who is still at home becomes more relaxed, and daily life can be easier to cope with.

▼ *It's great to be able to comfort your parents when they are feeling low, but you shouldn't feel it's up to you to solve their problems.*

Often, one or both parents will be sad and angry and their children may see them crying or hear them shouting on the phone. This can be very hard for children to deal with, especially if they are feeling upset themselves. The children may feel that it is up to them to make their Mum or Dad feel better. However, it is important to realize that adults need to sort their feelings out for themselves. Children should be able to get on with enjoying their own lives as much as possible.

In the early days after a split, children often feel very torn between their parents. They may want to take sides and get very angry with their Mum or Dad. This is a natural reaction, but it's much better for everyone if children don't get involved in their parents' arguments. When children join in a row, everyone becomes much more upset.

In some families the break-up doesn't happen straight away. One partner may move out for a short while and then come back again. This can be very unsettling for the children, who don't know whether their parents will end up together or apart.

'The first few weeks after Dad left felt really weird. Mum was crying a lot of the time, and I was trying hard to cheer her up. In the end I realized I couldn't do much to make her feel better. So I went out for the afternoon with my friend and then brought her home with me for supper. Actually, that seemed to cheer Mum up a lot.'

Laura, 14

▼ *After a marriage split-up, children may need to help more around the house.*

Where will I live?

When a family splits up, decisions need to be made about where the children will spend their time.

Some separated parents make arrangements for their children to spend half their time in one parent's house and half in the other's. This works especially well when parents live close to each other so that their children can move easily from one house to the other. In many other separated families, the children spend weekdays with one parent, and visit their other parent at the weekends and in the school holidays. But each family is different – what matters most is that both parents continue to play an important part in their children's lives.

▼ *Some children spend weekdays at their Mum's house and visit their Dad at the weekends and in the holidays.*

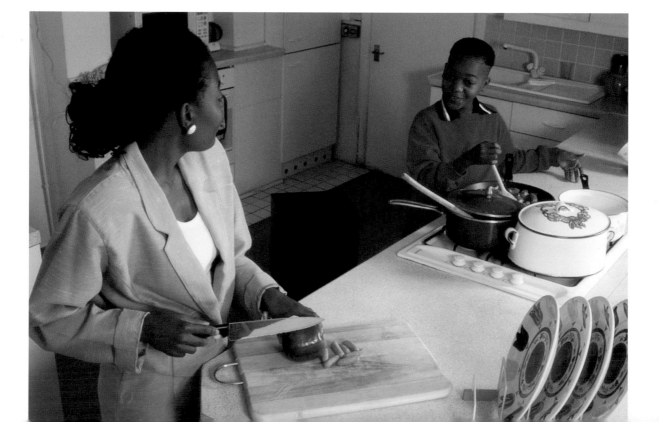

case study · case study · case study · case study · case study

Peter and Lucy live with their Dad during the week. He is a designer who works from home, so he can take them to school and look after them in the evenings. Their Mum is a nurse who often works nights. They go to stay with her at the weekends and spend a lot of their holidays with her.

Sadly, not all parents manage to agree about where their children should live. Sometimes couples have to go to court so that a judge can decide on which parent the children should live with, and when and where they should see the other parent. The judge's job is to make the best possible arrangements for the children. Whenever possible, this will often involve both parents spending some time with their children.

▲ In some separated families, the father is the parent who looks after the children most of the time.

A new way of life

It can take quite a long time to get used to living with just one parent instead of two. Most children miss doing special things with their Mum or their Dad. After a family breaks up, many single parents move to a smaller house or a flat. Usually, both parents have less money than before, so they may need to spend more time at work than they used to.

▲ *Single-parent families generally have less money to spend on food than families with two parents.*

FACT:
During the 1990s, the US National Bureau of Economic Research conducted a survey of family incomes before and after divorce. They studied the family income of children whose parents had divorced and remained divorced for at least six years. During this time, the income of the family fell by 40 to 45 per cent. The food consumption of the family was also reduced by 17 per cent.

Sometimes single parents can be very tired at the end of the day. They may also need more help around the house. In some cases, the children can feel that their Mum or Dad is just too tired and busy to spend time with them, but sometimes the opposite is true. Many young people find that after their parents split up, they have a chance to get to know their Mum and Dad really well. Instead of arguing with their partner all the time, each parent has more time and energy to do enjoyable things with their children.

weblinks

For more information about living in a single-parent family, go to www.waylinks.co.uk/series/why/familybreakup

Many children don't manage to see as much of both their parents as they would like, and, in a few cases, one parent disappears entirely from their lives. When this happens, it's natural for children to feel very sad and to miss that parent.

▼ *Some separated parents find they have more time to spend having fun with their children.*

Seeing both parents

Many young people live with one parent but visit the other one regularly. This arrangement can work very well, but there can also be problems. Sometimes, young people feel disappointed that they are not in the place they want to be. Perhaps there is a party close to their Mum's house while they are away for the weekend with their Dad. In situations like this, it's good for the children to tell their parents how they feel. Sometimes it might be possible to rearrange the dates of a visit. However, many young people decide that it's worth giving up a few parties in order to spend some time with their other parent.

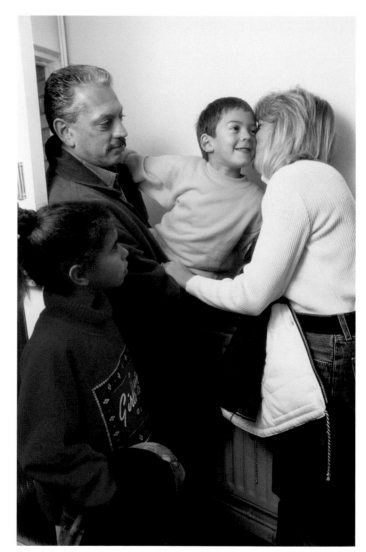

▲ For many children, swapping between two houses is just a normal part of life.

Sometimes, one parent will give their children lots of expensive presents and treats. This is a way of showing their love for their children, but it can be very hard for the other parent to watch this happening, especially if they do not have a lot of money to spend on their children. They may start to feel jealous and angry that they cannot give the children treats too.

Many separated parents manage to cooperate very well together. But, sadly, there are cases where the children feel that they are caught in the middle of their parents' rows. Sometimes parents complain to their children about the things the other parent does. They may ask questions about their ex-partner's life and even suggest that the children pass on messages. This can be very upsetting for the children involved. Young people should never be expected to take sides in their parents' arguments.

FACT:
In 1991, about 20 million children in the United States lived with just one parent. This is 28 per cent of all US children. Of these, the vast majority (84 per cent) lived with their mother.

◀ It's great to have fun with your Dad – especially if you don't see him very much because he's separated from your Mum – but sometimes there can be problems over too many presents or treats.

New partners

After a couple has been apart for a while, one or both of them may find a new partner. This can be difficult for their children to cope with. Although the children may be happy that their Mum or Dad has found someone new, they will probably also feel sad, because there is now very little chance that their parents will ever get back together again.

case study · case study · case study

Jon and his Mum had been living on their own for a year when she met Paul. At first Jon was angry about Paul. Jon was the one who looked after his Mum now and they didn't need anyone else in their life. Jon also didn't like it when Paul told him that it was time to go to bed. Jon talked to his Mum about his feelings, and Paul stopped telling him what to do. They started playing football and computer games together and Jon decided it was fun having Paul around.

▼ *It can be hard to get used to another adult telling you what to do.*

It can be hard to get used to having another adult in your life. In particular, many young people resent it when someone who is not their parent tells them what to do. In these situations, it's a good idea for children to talk to their Mum or Dad, and tell them what's making them unhappy. Sometimes it just takes time to get used to a

parent's new partner. But after a while, young people may find that they like having the new man or woman around. Of course, they know that the new partner will never replace their real Mum or Dad, but they can still enjoy having fun together.

▲ Eventually, you may start to enjoy having your parent's new partner around.

6. Moving on

Looking ahead

Although there are many things that take a long time to adjust to, there comes a time when separated families begin to settle down into their new way of life. Parents become less upset and angry and children get used to their new routines.

weblinks

For more information about what it is like to live in a stepfamily, go to www.waylinks.co.uk/series/why/familybreakup

Eventually, one or both parents might marry again and there may be stepbrothers and stepsisters to get to know. This can be a very big challenge for all the children involved. It can be very hard to get along with other children, and to share your Mum or Dad with someone else.

▲ *Some stepfamilies work really well, and everyone has fun and enjoys being with one another.*

Sometimes, stepbrothers and stepsisters never really get on well, and nobody should feel guilty about this. However, some stepfamilies work very well, and the young people have lots of good times together.

Many young people will have a new half-brother or half-sister, as their Mum or Dad has a baby with their new partner. This can be a very exciting time, but it is also possible to feel left out. It's good to talk to your family about how you are feeling about the new baby.

Whatever happens in your family, there will be new challenges to face. After a while, you will stop looking back and thinking so much about the past, and start to think about the future instead.

'We met Sarah and her boys when Mum and Dad had been divorced for two years. We usually saw them for part of the weekend when we were visiting Dad. We got on really well with the boys and at first I thought that Sarah was just a family friend. When I realized that she was Dad's girlfriend, I was really pleased. Now Dad and Sarah have been married for five years, and all of us kids get on really well together.'

Alex, 13

▼ *Getting to know your new stepbrother or stepsister can be a rewarding experience.*

Feeling better now

As time passes, things usually get much easier for everyone in the family. Most young people stop feeling so sad and start having fun with their friends again.

However, although daily life definitely gets better, there can be times when it feels bad again. On special occasions, such as birthdays and Christmas, it can feel sad not to have both parents together, and family holidays with just one parent can seem strange. There are also stages in a young person's life when they really miss having their other parent around. For example, as they reach puberty, they may wish that they could talk to a parent of the same sex about the changes they are going through.

◀ It's great to have your Mum around to give you advice, and if she's not there, it's only natural that you will miss her.

Or perhaps, if there is a problem in their life, they will miss being able to talk to a parent who 'would have known exactly what to say'.

But despite these difficult times, many young people look back on their family break-up and realize that it may have been the best thing for everyone. They recognize that their parents were very unhappy together and that they couldn't continue to live as they were. Of course, the children of separated parents will always feel sad that their parents had to part, but, as time passes, they will probably be able to feel much calmer about it.

> ' 'Being with Mum and Dad now, I can tell that they are both much happier than they were two years ago.
> It's been very hard living through the divorce, but I think we're all looking forward to the future now.'
> *Kate, 14*

▼ *Once everything has settled down after a family break-up, it feels good to relax and enjoy life again, perhaps with a new step-parent as part of the family.*

GLOSSARY

Abuse
To treat a person cruelly, either physically or verbally, or both.

Addicted
Unable to give up something, such as alcohol, tobacco or drugs.

Adjust
To get used to something, as in being well adjusted to a situation.

Bankrupt
Having no money, unable to pay debts.

Communication
Sharing thoughts and feelings, talking to other people.

Concentrate
To focus your thoughts closely on something, such as work or a book.

Consumption
The amount of food used up or eaten.

Cooperate
To work together with someone else.

Counsellor
Someone who has been trained to listen to other people's problems and who tries to give good advice to help them.

Criticize
To tell someone what is wrong with them or what they have done wrong.

Disagreements
Arguments.

Divorce
The official ending of a marriage by a law court.

Emotions
Strong feelings, such as happiness, love, sadness, anger.

Ex-partner
Someone who used to be a partner, husband or wife.

Fire
To tell someone that they must leave their job.

Helpline
A telephone service where people offer help and advice to people who ring in.

Irritable
Grumpy and bad-tempered.

Non-communication
Keeping thoughts and feelings to yourself, bottling things up inside.

Nuclear family
A family where the parents and their children all live together.

Numb
Unable to feel anything.

Partner
A husband, wife or permanent companion.

Professional
Someone who is specially trained to do a job, and who is paid to do it.

Puberty
The time, normally during early teenage years, when your body changes from a child's to an adult's.

Reaction
A feeling you have because of something that has happened to you.

Redundant
No longer needed for a job.

Refuge
A safe place.

Relationship
The way in which two people get on together.

Resent
To feel hurt or angry about something, or to be offended by the action of someone else.

Responsibility
A duty to do something.

Slanging match
An argument in which each person calls the other bad names.

Social worker
Someone who is trained and employed to do social work, such as visiting people with problems and trying to help them.

Stepbrother/sister
The son or daughter of your mother or father's new partner.

Stepfamily
The family of your mother or father's new husband or wife, if they remarry.

Sympathetic
Understanding about someone else's troubles, feeling in sympathy with someone else.

Unconditional
Not depending on anything else, with no strings attached.

Withdraw
To stay away from other people and be quiet and shy.

FURTHER INFORMATION

BOOKS TO READ

Non-fiction
Caught In The Middle: Teenagers Talk About Their Parents' Divorce by Alys Swan Jackson (Piccadilly Press, 1997)
Divorce Happens To The Nicest Kids: A Self-Help Guide for Kids by Michael S. Prokop (Alegra House, 1996)
Mike's Lonely Summer – A Child's Guide Through Divorce by Carolyn Nystrom (Lion, 1994)
What Children Need To Know When Parents Get Divorced by William L. Coleman (Bethany House, 1998)
Wise Guides: Family Break-up by Matt Whyman (Hodder Children's Books, 2005)

Fiction
It's Not The End of the World by Judy Blume (Simon and Schuster, 2001)
Rescuing Dad by Peter Johnson (Corgi Yearling, 2001)
The Suitcase Kid by Jacqueline Wilson (Doubleday, 2001)

USEFUL CONTACTS

Childline
A free and confidential service for young people who are worried about personal problems,
like violence in the home, abuse or bullying.
Tel: 0800 1111
Textphone service: 0800 400 222

Relate
An agency that provides advice and counselling for couples and families.
Relate Central Office is at:
Herbert Gray College,
Little Church Street,
Rugby,
Warwickshire CV21 3AP
Tel: (lo-call) 0845 456 1310 or 01788 573241
Fax: 01788 535007

WEBSITES
For websites that are relevant to this book, go to www.waylinks.co.uk/series/why/familybreakup

INDEX

Numbers in **bold** refer to pictures.

abuse 21, **21**, 46
addiction 20, 46
adjusting 46
alcohol 20, **20**, 21
anger 24, 25, 38, 42
arguments 12, **12**, 13, **13**, 17, 27, 28, 32, 33, 37, 39
Australia 5

babies, new 19, **19**, 43
bankruptcy 16, 46
birthdays 44

Childline 21
children 13, 21, 22, 26, 27, 28, 29, 30, 32, 33, 34, 35, 36, 37, 38, 39, 40, 42
Christmas 44
comforting parents 32, **32**, 33
communication 7, 14, 15, 22, **23**, 25, **25**, 30, 31, 46
cooperation 39, 46
coping methods 14
counselling 22, **22**, 23, **23**
counsellors 20, 22, **22**, 23, 30, 46
courts 35
criticism 13, 46

death in family 16, 17, **17**
divorce 4, 5, 11, 21, 36, 43, 45, 46
divorce, effect on family income 36
divorce rates 5, 31
drink problems 20, **20**, 21
drug addiction 20

emotions when a family splits up 24, **24**, 25, 26, **26**, 27, 32, 33, 37

family, death in 17, **17**
family, having fun as a 8, **8**
financial problems 16, 36
friends, talking to 25, **24**, **25**, 30, **31**

guilt, feelings of 27, 28, **28**, 29

half-brothers 43
half-sisters 43
helplines 21, 46
holidays **8**, 44

illness 16, 17
individual pursuits 7, **7**

jealousy 38
jobs, losing 16, **16**

living with one parent 33, **33**, 34, **34**, 35, **35**, 36, **36**, 37, **37**, 38, 39, 44

marriage 4, **4**, 5, **5**, 6, 10, **15**
missing a parent 36, 37, 44, **44**, 45
money worries 12, 16, 19, 36, **36**
moving house 9, 16, 18, **18**, 19, 36

non-communication 14, **14**, **15**, 46
nuclear families 5, 46

parent leaving home 28, **28**, 32, 33
partners, new 40, **40**, 41, **41**
problems in family 16
puberty 44, 46

redundancy 16
refuges 21, **21**, 46
remarriage 42

resentment, feelings of 41
rows in family 12, **12**, 13, **13**, 17, 27, 28, 32, 33, 37, 39

sadness 24, **24**, 32
schoolwork 26, **26**
shock **26**
single-parent families 36, 37, 39
social workers 20, 46
splitting up 10, 11, 12, 13, 15, 21, 24, 26, 27, 28, 32, 33
stepbrothers 42, 43, **43**
stepfamilies 42, **42**, 43, **45**, 46
stepsisters 42, 43, **43**
stress 9, **9**, 19, 28, 29, **29**

taking sides 33, 39
talking to friends 25, **24**, **25**, 30, **31**
teachers 30
treats 38, **39**

United Kingdom 5, 21
United States 5, 31, 39
US National Bureau of Economic Research 36

violence, domestic 20, 21, **21**
visiting a parent 38

wedding day 4, **4**
women's refuges 21, **21**

young couples 11, **11**